Paul's Sauce

by Howard Lee
illustrated by Liz Callen

Core Decodable 98

McGraw Hill Education

Bothell, WA • Chicago, IL • Columbus, OH • New York, NY

MHEonline.com

Send all inquiries to:
McGraw-Hill Education
8787 Orion Place
Columbus, OH 43240

ISBN: 978-0-02-145291-0
MHID: 0-02-145291-1

Printed in the United States of America.

9 10 11 12 KOD 24

Paul likes to cook. He makes sauce. Because he likes it, he makes a lot.

Paul starts at dawn. He makes sauce all day. He yawns at night. But he still makes sauce.

Paul uses sauce a lot. He mixes it with noodles and meat. That is fine.

But Paul mixes sauce with cereal and raw beets. That tastes awful!

Paul mixes his sauce with straw for the cows.

Paul's cat gets saucers of sauce. The cat has sauce on its paws!

Paul makes jars and jars of sauce. I saw them in his basement and in his laundry.

Paul, stop making sauce!